The Brass Eagle Lecterns of England

Marcus van der Meulen

AMBERLEY

About the Author

Marcus van der Meulen studied Architecture and Interior Architecture at Leuven University and Monument Preservation at the Institute for Conservation and Restoration in Ghent, Belgium. At Cambridge University he took courses in Architectural History. His interest in churches started at an early age, visiting the English cathedrals during summer holidays and conducting family trips to village churches. During his studies he was a guide at St Bavo's Cathedral in Ghent.

Marcus researches the reactivation of religious heritage as a preservation strategy and studies church interiors. He is a member of the Ghirardacci Centre of Studies, Bologna, the Society of Study of the Church Interior and a member of the FRH (Future for Religious Heritage) Network and Communications committees.

First published 2017

Amberley Publishing
The Hill, Stroud
Gloucestershire, GL5 4EP

www.amberley-books.com

Copyright © Marcus van der Meulen, 2017

The right of Marcus van der Meulen to be identified as the Author
of this work has been asserted in accordance with the
Copyrights, Designs and Patents Act 1988.

All rights reserved. No part of this book may be reprinted
or reproduced or utilised in any form or by any electronic,
mechanical or other means, now known or hereafter invented,
including photocopying and recording, or in any information
storage or retrieval system, without the permission in writing
from the Publishers.

British Library Cataloguing in Publication Data.
A catalogue record for this book is available from the British Library.

ISBN 978 1 4456 6820 8 (print)
ISBN 978 1 4456 6821 5 (ebook)

Typeset in 11pt on 15pt Sabon.
Origination by Amberley Publishing.
Printed in the UK.

Contents

Introduction	5
Brass Eagle Lecterns in England	8
History and the Change of Function	17
Form and Meaning	29
Material and Production	39
Brass Eagle Lecterns in England	48
Origin of the Late Medieval and Early Modern Lecterns	76
Conclusion	85
List of Brass Eagle Lecterns	92
Bibliography	94

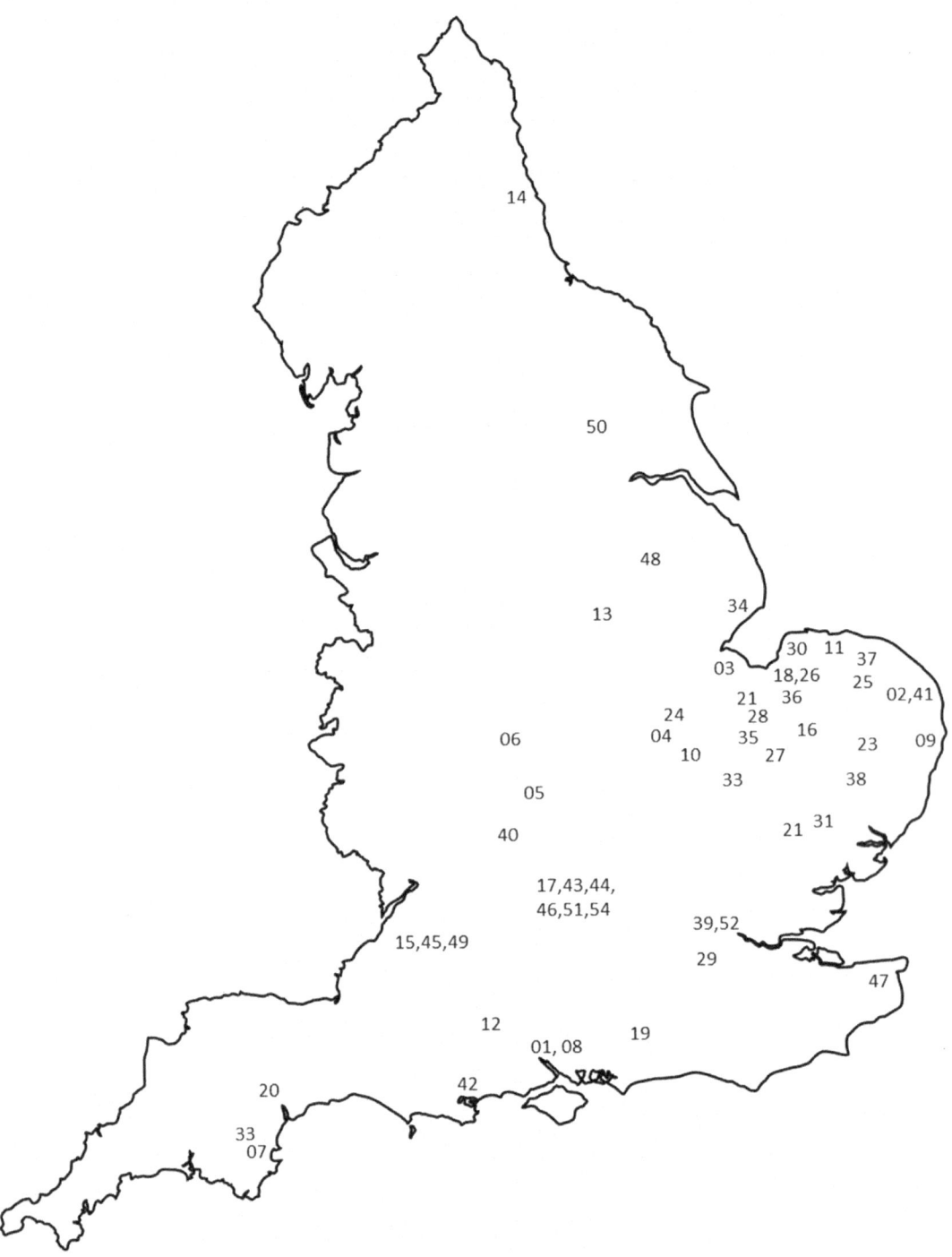

A map showing the distribution of brass eagle lecterns in England.

Introduction

During the late Victorian period, eagle lecterns were industrially produced.

The eagle lectern in Ely Cathedral is a Victorian copy of the one found in the fens outside Isleham, Cambridgeshire, in the 1830s.

The marshes on the outskirts of a village or the bottom of a local stream may seem to be an unlikely spot to find the ecclesiastical, yet it is in places like these that some of the finest examples of English brass eagle lecterns were found. Draining the fens outside Isleham in 1831 recovered a lectern that now shines in all its glory in the local church of St Andrew. The dredging of the river outside Oundle in the early nineteenth century produced a latten lectern of the late fifteenth century; in Devon a brass eagle was found in the woods and in Norfolk one was found in the churchyard. How these lecterns ended up in these godforsaken places is not always known and the origin of them often remains clouded by legends. Heavenly handouts to the faithful from above and divine provenance can be ruled out; these godly gifts were handmade – even the material the lecterns were produced from is manmade. Unlike wood or stone, brass is not found in nature, and the process of brass-making involved profound knowledge of metallurgy. Early accounts in medieval manuscripts make the process of brass-making sound like an alchemist's quest to produce gold. Indeed, the bookstand with its reading desk shaped like an eagle feels gothic. The description of Folcuin's head-turning latten bird with expendable wings, blowing frankincense out of its beak, only increases this sense of wonder. It would feel perfectly at home at Hogwarts. At Redenhall, the fantastical is cast in metal with an eagle looking to the north and the south simultaneously with its two heads. These mysterious creatures that had found their way inside the medieval churches were thrown out as sacrilegious objects of idolatry in the early modern period. Puritans despised this opulence and heresy. Many brass eagle lecterns ended up in the melting pot; others were mutilated while some could be hidden. The survival of any of these objects can be regarded a little miracle in itself.

Then came the revival for anything gothic; Mary Shelly's *Frankenstein* was published when the ancient furnishings suddenly reappeared from the bottom of a lake or dug up at a churchyard. Only a few decades later brass eagle lecterns were produced on an industrial scale never seen before – a massive output of reproductions filling Anglican churches throughout the country with near identical creatures. Once the outcome of skilled craftsmanship, the brass eagle lectern had suddenly become an object of mass production. The magic, however, of the English Lecterns – as the group of eagles made before the English Reformation is often referred to – has not diminished.

This book is the result of thorough research, visits, and conversations, and I would like to thank all who have played a part in it. A special thanks to Dr Ludovic Nys for his beneficial criticism, which has been supportive; Dr Julian Litten FSA; Dr Monique de Ruette; the Revd Canon Jonathan Baker; Jenifer Hawks of Art Alive in Churches; Crispin Truman OBE; Dr Justin Kroesen for providing marvelous shots of the eagle lectern in St Bride's Fleet Street; and my family, for their support.

Brass Eagle Lecterns in England

Durham Cathedral, late nineteenth century photography showing the pelican lectern by Sir George Gilbert Scott and Francis Skidmore in the location it was conceived for.

Truro Cathedral towards the reredos in the late nineteenth century.

In Truro Cathedral, an impressive brass bookstand draws the attention of the visitors when nearing the crossing of this Gothic Revival building. An elaborate piece of furniture, decorated with pious statuettes and organic foliage cast in latten, a fearsome eagle supports a reading desk and two candleholders to illuminate the scriptures. For the newly created Cornish cathedral, a magnificent lectern was created in the late nineteenth century to adorn its interior. By that time the brass eagle lectern had secured a firm place in the Anglican church interior. The Gothic Revival of the nineteenth century, with a renewed interest in the ecclesiastical space before the English Reformation, instigated a process of beautification. Hereford Cathedral was remodeled with a screen and in Durham the lost pelican lectern was replaced by a new creation, both designed by Sir George Gilbert Scott and made by Francis Skidmore of Coventry. Later generations showed less enthusiasm for some of these Victorian additions; at Hereford the screen was even removed, and the lavish bookstands were relocated. Only contemporary photographs provide a sight of the intended effect. At Durham and Truro, the impressive lectern was originally placed at the entrance of the choir in front of the screen looking down the aisle, at the end of a processional path. This is the location these furnishings where conceived for.

The Victorian beautification of the church interior was highly influenced by the Oxford Movement and the Cambridge Camden Society. Gothic Revival was to dominate the ecclesiastical architecture of the period. From ancient cathedrals to newly erected places of worship, the church interiors were gothic. The beautified ecclesiastical space and renewed interest in liturgy resulted in a revival of the brass eagle lectern – an ancient bookstand that was both lavish and functional. At Truro, the impressive eagle lectern took inspiration from the gothic examples dating back to the fifteenth and early sixteenth centuries. One of the finest of these was found at Oscott College, Birmingham. Today this brass marvel is one of the treasures at the Cloisters in New York, but for little over a century the lectern had been at the Roman Catholic seminary. It had been presented for the inauguration of St Chad's Cathedral, Birmingham, by the Earl of Shrewsbury. Designed by Augustus W. N. Pugin, this house of worship was decorated with authentic pre-Reformation furnishings. The Victorians had observed the Oscott Lectern for its lavish design. It became an instant inspiration for the restoration of the pelican lectern of Norwich Cathedral and for the creation of new elaborate lecterns for Truro or Durham Cathedrals. At that time, the Catholic liturgical

The early sixteenth-century eagle lectern once in Pugin's Cathedral of St Chad, Birmingham.

St Chad's Cathedral, Birmingham, (1839–1841) by Augustus A. W. Pugin. To adorn its Gothic Revival interior, the Earl of Shrewsbury acquired the impressive eagle lectern.

object had become an Anglican church fitting. Many Anglican churches had a more modest bookstand in the form of an eagle placed on a simpler stem and pedestal. Hart, Son & Peard of London, Jones & Willis of Birmingham, Benham & Froud of London and all other suppliers of ecclesiastical fittings produced their versions of the brass eagle lectern and looked at the gothic examples for inspiration. The Victorian lectern at Ely Cathedral fits perfectly between its older counterparts at Long Sutton, Walpole St Peter or Outwell.

Some suppliers made replicas. At Thoverton, in the south-east of England, the bookstand is a copy of a lectern found in King's Lynn, Norfolk. At times the Gothic Revival becomes a simple reproduction of the earlier examples. Anglican churches all over the country were filled with the lavish bookstands, now mass produced and transported by rail. This massive output on an industrial scale, only rivalled by the production of the late fifteenth and early sixteenth century, has cast a spell on all Victorian metalwork. Objects such as the Hereford Screen or the Pelican Lectern by Sir George Gilbert and Francis Skidmore are unique works of art and deserve to be appreciated as such.

Of the fifty plus brass eagle lecterns dating before the Gothic Revival, an astounding forty or so are early modern. Only one can be called medieval and, of the Georgian Period, only two survive to this day. The others were made in the seventeenth century and, unsurprisingly, none during the Commonwealth.

During the Victorian Era the brass eagle lectern was revived. Cathedrals, churches and college chapels throughout the country were adorned with these ecclesiastical fittings. Here, the Gothic Revival Chapel of Selwyn College, Cambridge. (Photography David Iliff)

The lectern in St Bride Fleet Street, London.

Brasenose College Chapel, Oxford. (Photography David Iliff)

History and the Change of Function

More than a hundred years since the casting of the last eagle had passed. Made for Brasenose College, Oxford, the brazen bird presented by Thomas Lee Drummer in 1731 concluded a tradition going back centuries. After the English Reformation, only a dozen or so were cast; memorials placed in college chapels and fittings to stage a High Church liturgy. At Canterbury, the latten bookstand made by William Borroughes in 1662 replaced an earlier example that had been a victim of vicious iconoclasm. The cathedral was ransacked in 1642 by Colonel Sandys's troops, but the Canterbury lectern was not the only eagle that suffered during the Civil War; blasphemy in the House of the Lord, the brass eagle had become a golden calf in the eyes of many a Puritan. Some were hidden in a nearby river, others in the woods or were buried in the churchyard, all to protect them from harsh atrocities. Several were only recovered in the early nineteenth century, at a time when the interest in these ancient fittings was growing.

The Puritan cleansing came after a revival of the brass eagle lectern in the early Stuart period. Named after William Laud, the Archbishop of Canterbury, the Laudian Revival of the 1630s and 1640s celebrated the beauty of holiness. As a reaction to the austerity of the Elizabethan Church, a High Church liturgy commenced in some cathedrals and college chapels in Oxford and Cambridge. At Wimborne Minster, the church was refurbished, first with a rood screen and stalls in 1610, and a brass eagle lectern completed the redecoration of the ecclesiastical space in 1623. An interesting example is the adornment of the church in Little Gidding, Huntingdonshire. The Elizabethan Church had been Calvinist – even the organ was treated with suspicion. Similar to the resurrection of organs in some college chapels, Magdalen in Oxford and St John's in Cambridge are good examples.

WILLIAM LORD ARCHBISHOP OF CANterbury his grace, Primate of all England and Metropolitane and Chancelour of the Vniuersity of Oxford &c.

Right: The reform in the Anglican Church of the early seventeenth century is named Laudianism after William Laud, the Archbishop of Canterbury (1633–1645). During this period the church interior witnessed a cautious revival of embellishment.

Below: Wimborne Minster in Dorset. In the early seventeenth century this former monastic church was refurbished, including what was perhaps the first brass eagle lectern made after the English Reformation.

Drawn by W. Waller.   Engraved by J. Fisher.

N.W. VIEW OF WIMBORNE MINSTER CHURCH.

The minute church in Little Gidding was embellished with an instrument to beautify the service and, like Wimborne Minster, the interior was adorned with a brazen lectern. An early Tudor example – a subtle reference to pre-Reformation times perhaps – was acquired by Nicholas Ferrar and presented to this Anglican High Church laboratory. Little Gidding has become an example of the rebirth in the Anglican Church of liturgy and, consequently, of rich church furnishings.

Often lecterns were presented to the church as a memorial. The names of the benefactors are inscribed and recalled, if not polished away by later generations. In St Mary Redcliffe, Bristol, the sphere on which the eagle rests recollects the name of John Wathen and the date 1638. At Balliol College, Oxford, the pre-Reformation bookrest shows the date it was presented to the college chapel, prompting some to interpret this is the date the lectern was made. The initials 'A. W.' are engraved on the bookstand at Wimborne Minster, most likely standing for Anthony Wayte, who is buried in the near

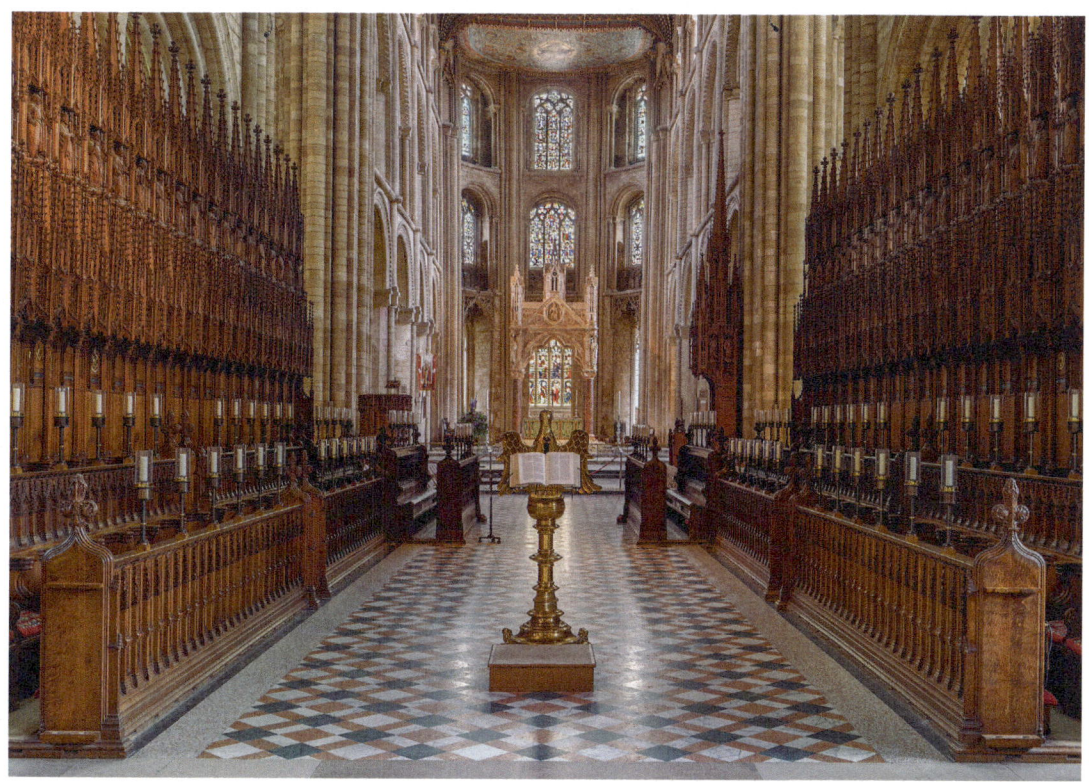

The brass eagle lectern has been part of the ecclesiastical furnishings at Peterborough Cathedral since the late fifteenth century. (Photography David Iliff)

The Abbot and Prior of the Abbey of St Peter, St Paul and St Andrew at Peterborough were the benefactors of the late fifteenth-century lectern.

vicinity of the lectern. The bookstands in college chapels and collegiate churches often were commemorations and monuments to their benefactors. With an exception perhaps of some of the cathedral lecterns, the specimens of the seventeenth and eighteenth centuries were intended as memorials, albeit functional fixtures, engraved with initials or full names on a spot visible for all. This was a reconnection to an older tradition of donating liturgical fittings as commemorative furnishings. Several lecterns from the fifteenth and early sixteenth centuries bear the names of their benefactors. At Peterborough Cathedral the lectern was presented by its abbot and prior, and their names were recorded before the engraving became illegible. At the end of the fifteenth century, not only clergymen donated this liturgical object as their memorial. William Westbrok and his wives Rose and Johanne are remembered by the lectern now in St Giles', Norwich. '*Orate pro anima*', the inscription in Latin commences, 'pray for the souls of the patrons', in anticipation of the promised eternal life after death.

Henry VIII did not anticipate an alteration of the church interior when he broke away from Rome. This process only gradually developed as the Reformation in England advanced. The dissolution of the monasteries meant an abrupt end for many brass lecterns, which had been part of the fittings of monastic houses. Peterborough Abbey was made a cathedral, safeguarding the exceptional lectern in this magnificent environment for 500 years, but this is a rare if not unique exception. The latten bookstands of the seventeenth and early eighteenth centuries were made to support a copy of the Bible in the English language – a function the lectern received during the Reformation. The English Reformation had come with a transformation of the liturgy and alterations of the ecclesiastical space accordingly. During the reign of Henry VIII, the Bible was translated into the common language; before that time, readings from the scriptures were in Latin, in the chancel, which was incomprehensible for the masses.

From 1538 the English Bible had to be displayed for consultation in the nave of the church. A reading desk was required, preferably a bookstand where the book could be chained for security reasons – in a way a continuation of the medieval monastic library. The eagle lectern could fulfil this function perfectly and some were relocated from the chancel to a place closer to the congregation. In Havering church, Greater London, Edward VI's inventory of 1554 describes 'an Egle of latten whiche ys to leye the bible on'. At St Petrock's Church in Exeter, the bookrest was relocated in 1560 to 'the body of the church, to set the bible on'. The translation into the common language had brought the bible closer to the congregation and the relocation of the lectern from chancel – the area behind the rood screen or pulpitum reserved for the clergy – to the 'body of the church' situated the Bible closer to the community. This is where many eagles in parish churches can be found today – placed before the screen, not hidden away in the chancel. The church of St Peter, St Paul and St Thomas of Canterbury in Bovey Tracey, Devon, is a fine example.

Although the Bible regained a much more central position in the Ecclesia Anglicana, the brass eagle as its support was not seen appropriate by all. In Westminster Abbey the chapter orders the two brass lecterns present to be sold, as they are 'monuments to idolatry and superstition'. A systematic campaign to undo the Anglican church interior from this idolatry was never attempted; several church wardens, however, chose to replace the latten bookstand by another of a cheaper material, like wood. At Long Melford, Suffolk, the medieval Rood Cross was used to fabricate one. Of the hundred

REDUCED FAC-SIMILE OF THE TITLE-PAGE OF THE GREAT BIBLE.

Above and opposite: Henry VIII handing out the Great Bible, in print and translated into the English language.

or so brass eagle lecterns known from inventories in 1536, less than half survive, many having ended up in the melting pot. In the City of London, the church of St Christopher-le-Stocks sold their 'egle of latten' in 1581. *Pecunia non olet*.

Records from King's Lynn reveal the pre-Reformation church could have up to three lecterns. Not all bookstands were made of brass; other materials were also used like metal or stone and mostly wood. A fine example of a wooden lectern, common at the time yet a rarity today, can be found in Ranworth, Norfolk. It is a simple bookstand with two desks on different levels. At Durham Cathedral there were two lecterns – one in the shape of a pelican and another in the shape of an eagle. These bookstands had different functions. One was for reading from the Gospels – the four books by the four Evangelists describing the life, death and resurrection of Christ – while the other was used for reading from the Epistles – the letters written to early Christians by the Apostles. Both are part of the New Testament.

The location of these bookstands in the medieval church interior can differ. Usually, however, they are fixed to the *cornu evangelii* for Gospel reading and the *cornu epistolae* for the Epistle, in the chancel to the north

The medieval wooden lectern in Ranworth, Norfolk. (Photography Justin Kroesen and Regnerus Steensma)

and south of the altar. The eagle would always look east, the priest would have his back to the faithful when singing from the Gospel. 'There was a goodly fine letteron of brasse where they sunge the epistle and the gospell', recalls the sixteenth-century author of the *Rites of Durham*, a Tudor scroll describing the liturgy at the priory at the time before the Dissolution; sung, yet not in the common language but in Latin. Lecterns could also be used to display a large gradual or antiphonary used for choral singing. Some have double reading desks; King's College, Cambridge is perhaps the best known example – an impressive stand, crowned by a statuette of Henry VI, placed centrally between the stalls. But the brazen eagle could also be used for supporting musical books. Like the Gospels these were manuscripts, handwritten and decorated with illuminations. An Evangelarium was often regarded the most significant treasure of any church, the support of the word of God consequently being of immeasurable standing.

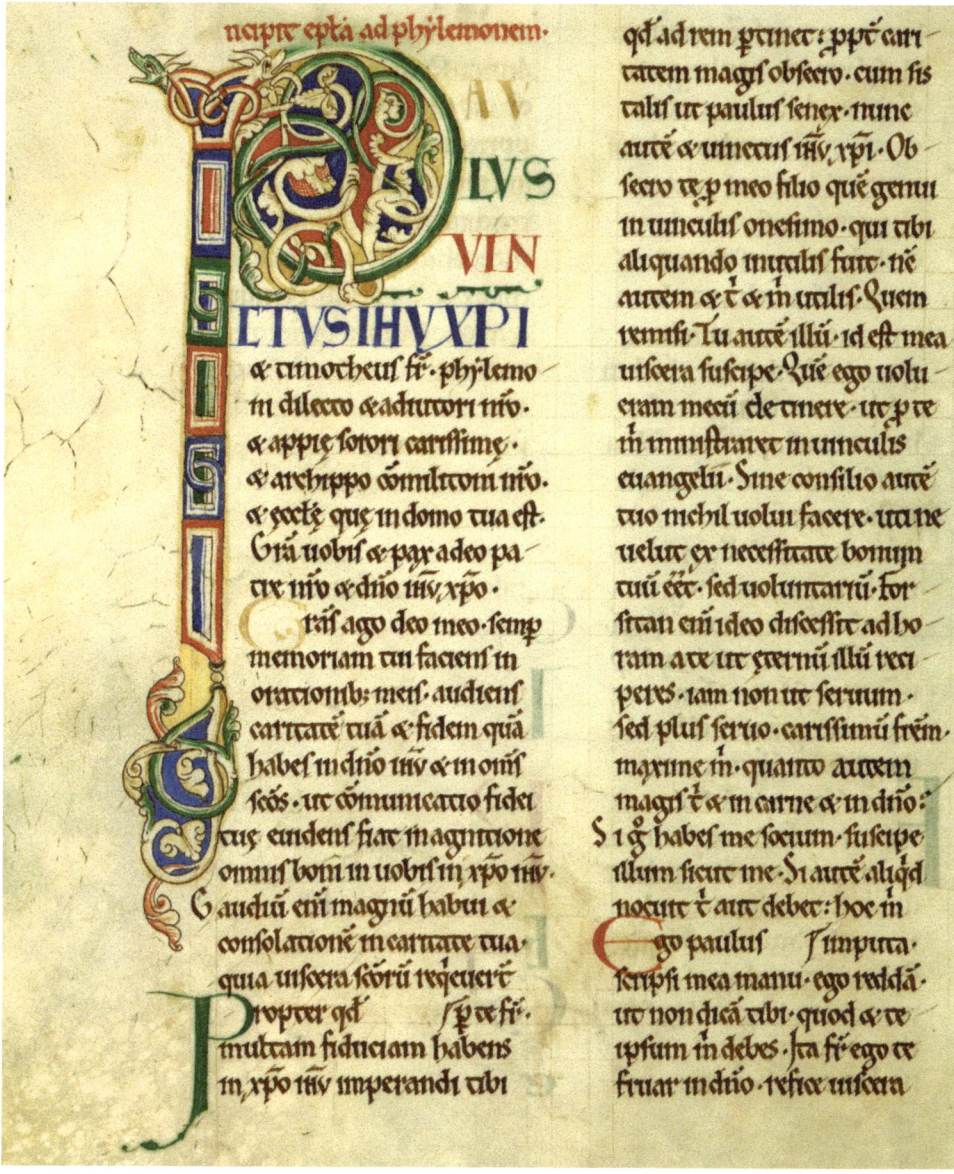

The Epistle of Philemon, Bible of Rochester Cathedral, first half of the twelfth century, English. Large books such as the Rochester Bible were placed on lecterns to chant the scriptures from.

Carrow Psalter, East Anglian, mid-thirteenth century.

Norwich Cathedral choir. (Photography David Iliff)

The first mention of a freestanding bookstand with a reading desk in the shape of an eagle dates from the tenth century. In 970, Folcuin of Lobbes had a lectern made to read the Gospels from, which was placed on the pulpitum of his abbey church. It was made of brass or bronze and its head could turn and accommodate frankincense, filling the church with incense through its open beak. There was even a device that enabled the wings to expand. Folcuin's lectern must have been a marvelous sight. The pulpitum is also the location of the liturgical bookstand mentioned in the inventory from 1592 of St Saviour's Minster in Utrecht; this freestanding support probably developed from eagles supporting reading desks that were part of the pulpitum. Some stone pulpits or large ambos of the early and high Middle Ages still feature these attachments. A fine example can be found in the Abbey of San Clemente a Casauria in Italy. It is in abbeys like Lobbes that the freestanding bookrest arrives first, then later in the High Middle Ages the cathedrals and collegiate churches followed. The wooden eagle lectern of Exeter Cathedral, dating from the fourteenth century, now in St Thomas, is a fine example. Inventories made during the Reformation reveal that most brass lecterns were part of the monastic houses, cathedrals, or collegiate churches.

Form and Meaning

Above and Previous page: The early sixteenth-century lectern at St Bride's Church, Fleet Street, City of London.

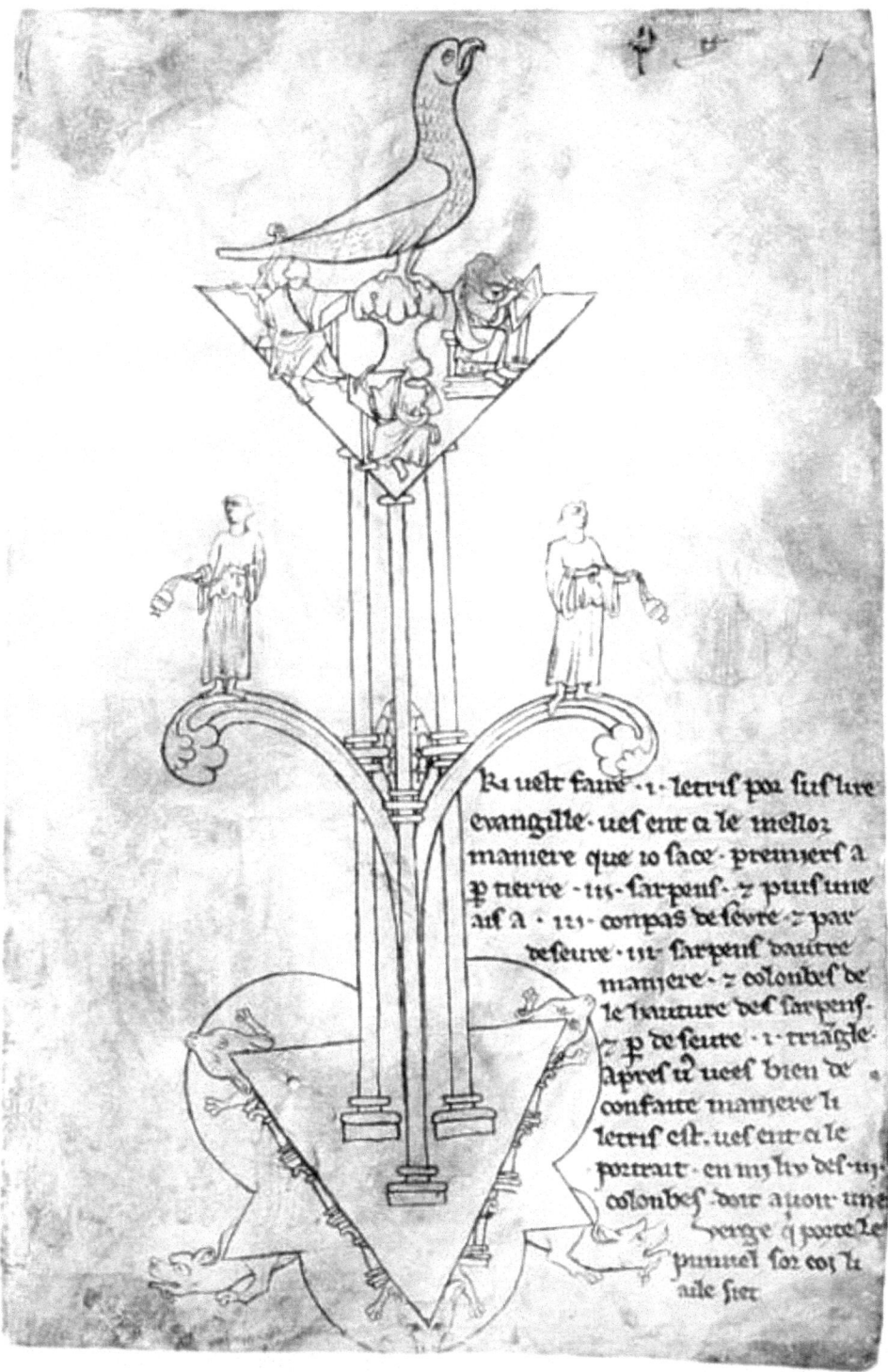

'For those who want to make a lectern to read the Gospels from,' from the sketchbook of Villard de Honnecourt, first half of the thirteenth century.

From the lavish lecterns in some cathedrals to the more modest bookstands in parish churches, the lectern consists of three parts: the reading desk, the stand, and the pedestal. This is how Villard de Honnecourt represents the eagle lectern in his sketchbook dating back to the early thirteenth century. By that time, this type of liturgical furniture had become a standard fitting for the gothic cathedral. With its wings widespread, the eagle in the drawing appears to be floating in the air, ascending to heaven. It is similar to the specimen from Holyrood Abbey in Southampton; dating from the late fourteenth century, this latten bookstand is the oldest eagle lectern in England. The stand can be executed as a stem or treated as a piece of miniature architecture, like the wooden example in Exeter. In the fifteenth century, a more abstract design for the stand becomes prevalent, a type that defines most later English brass lecterns. Simultaneously the pedestals become circular; the earlier gothic examples often show a triangular base. The drawing by Villard de Honnecourt shows a complex pedestal made up of geometrical forms. Supporting the pedestal are three serpents. Most lecterns have three or four feet in the shape of lions; these can be seated or *couchant*, lying with their heads looking to the right or the left. Occasionally other animals occur, such as dogs or serpents. Without exception the wings of the bird are widespread. Some are more plastic, others appear to be flat. The early modern eagles have wings that appear more abstract and can be divided into four or five types. Later eagles have more developed wings, growing increasingly more naturalistic. Perhaps the most developed eagle and certainly recognisable as this king of birds is the one in St Paul's Cathedral. The paws and claws of several early Tudor birds are thick and disproportionately large, and the talons, all individually cast, are very long and occasionally lacking. Later eagles from the seventeenth century have more slender paws and much shorter talons.

Some eagles are cast in the moment of flight, which is especially true for the older ones. Later birds appear to be floating in the sky, ready to ascend to heaven. Other birds take a resting pose standing on a pole. In Southampton, the Holyrood bird is caught in flight; this is later repeated with the examples in Lincoln and Canterbury. Early modern eagles can be cast as resting on the sphere rather than flying. The heads can be divided into two groups – either looking towards the sky or straight ahead – and a preference for the symmetrical remains prevalent until the nineteenth century. Medieval lecterns often feature a small demon on its back between the bird's paws. This feature is missing with the early modern lecterns and

Most brass lecterns are supported by three or four little lions, seated or couchant.

returns only sporadically during the Gothic Revival. In Norwich Cathedral the bird bows its head to pick its breast and is referred to as a pelican. Another pre-Reformation known example was at Durham Cathedral; the current pelican lectern is a Victorian replacement by Scott and Skidmore. This nineteenth-century example has candleholders attached to the lectern. None of the pre-Reformation lecterns have these candlesticks today, although it is said the Peterborough eagle had these taken off during the Civil War. The seventeenth-century examples in Canterbury and Lincoln do have candlesticks attached to the bird's wings.

In Christian iconography the eagle can have numerous connotations. One of these is as the symbol for St John the Evangelist. His Gospel famously commences with the words *In principio erat verbum*, 'In the beginning was the word'. At Ranworth, the wooden lectern depicts an eagle with a scroll in its beak repeating these first words from the Gospel according to John. In the written text accompanying his drawing, Villard de Honnecourt discloses the function of the eagle lectern as to read the Gospels from. The Gospels are part of the Bible describing the life, death and resurrection of Christ as

Above left: A sketch of a double-headed eagle lectern.

Above right: Common once but a rarity today is the medieval wooden lectern at Ranworth. (Photography Justin Kroesen and Regnerus Steensma)

written down by the four Evangelists Matthew, Mark, Luke and John. At Messina Cathedral, the impressive brass lectern, sadly lost in the devastating earthquake of 1908, had four rotating bookrests attached to it, supported by the four allegorical depictions of the Evangelists: Matthew as an angel, Mark as a lion, Luke as a bull, and John as the eagle, all four with scrolls. This tetramorph is again represented at the brass Paschal candleholder of Genoa Cathedral, dating back to the late fourteenth century. In combination with the other animals of Ezekiel, the eagle can undoubtedly be identified as a symbol for St John.

Reading the Gospels was one function of the lectern; the others were reading from the Epistle and a support for musical books. Contemporary

Form and Meaning

Above: The lost Evangelistario of Messina Cathedral displaying four desks.

Right: The Eagle as a symbol of St John the Evangelist.

images, such as one by Simon Bening, today in Waddesdon Manor, show a brass eagle lectern surrounded by choristers and choirboys, illustrating that this type of bookstand was not exclusively used for Gospel reading. At Norwich Cathedral, the reading desk is supported by a pelican. It is known the Duke of Burgundy had a lectern made for the ducal burial chapel that was topped by a phoenix. At Redenhall, Suffolk, the bookrest has the shape of a unique double-headed eagle. Iconography can reveal the meaning of these mythical animals. In *Physiologus* – a medieval book describing the world as an allegory of heaven – the pelican is described as the bird that picks its breast to feed its brood. This was seen as a reference to Christ's sacrifice and subsequently a symbol for the Eucharist. This quality made the bird a pelican rather than its physical appearance. A pelican became a recurrent theme in the decoration of the sacrament niche where the host was kept. The phoenix is a reference to the resurrection of Christ and thus a promise of life after death for all the faithful, and the double-headed eagle can also be interpreted as a symbol for Christ, either the double nature as both human and divine, or as the King of Heaven and Earth. The *Physiologus* also describes the eagle as an allegory for Christ. This correspondents to the meaning William Durand, the thirteenth-century Bishop of Mende and writer on liturgy, provides for the eagle supporting the reading desk. Without a scroll in its beak, the eagle can be interpreted as a representation of Christ, conforming to the meaning of the pelican and the double-headed eagle. The remarks made during the Reformation to undo the ecclesiastical space of its eagles of latten as they were blasphemous symbols of idolatry become understandable. The symbol of an eagle on a pole, however, goes back much further in history. Romans used the eagle with its wings widespread on top of their standards and the Aquila was a symbol for victory. In Greek mythology the eagle is a transformation of Zeus, king of the gods. As a symbol of victory of life over death, the eagle lectern became a symbol for the resurrection – Christ's triumph of life over death.

Form and Meaning

The Eagle as described in the *Physiologus*.

Brass candleholder with reading desk, Meuse Valley, fifteenth century.

By the fifteenth century, brass candlesticks were produced in series.

Material and Production

The late fifteenth-century lectern in Bovey Tracey, Devon. (Photography Justin Kroesen and Regnerus Steensma)

Scientifically speaking, latten or brass – the difference is purely linguistic – is an alloy of copper and zinc. The latter was unknown as a material in the western world until the seventeenth century; instead, a powdered stone containing high quantities of zinc ore called calamine was used. Brass objects had been made by the Romans but it was during the medieval period that the yellow-coloured metal became a popular material for candlesticks and cauldrons, kettles and candelabras. The production experienced a short-lived revival during the reign of Charlemagne, before brassmaking started to blossom from the tenth century onwards. Improved casting techniques as a result of contacts with Vikings are thought to be of importance.

Latten objects for domestic and liturgical use started to claim their place in all layers of society during the high Middle Ages. A description of brass in *De Mineralibus*, the book on minerals by Albertus Magnus dating back to the thirteenth century, is an early attempt to understand the alloy. The medieval professor describes the production of the metal and tries to comprehend the process of transformation from copper to brass. Albertus Magnus was most interested in this transmutation of one metal into a material resembling gold, yet lacking some of its essential qualities. In his description of the process, it approaches the work of an alchemist searching in his laboratory for a way to produce gold, rather than an understanding of metallurgy. The idea that brass was a cheap substitute for gold, however, is ill-founded. Latten objects such as eagle lecterns were luxury products and expensive fixtures; raw ingredients had their price and the manufacture of brass objects was a skilled craft.

Around 1120, Theophilus Presbyter wrote about brass production in his work *Schedula Diversarum Atrium (List of Various Arts)*. A thirteenth-century copy from Lincoln is now in the Cambridge University Library. Theophilus names the main ingredients as copper, charcoal and calamine – the stone containing high levels of zinc. The copper was heated in a crucible – a more or less closed vessel – and the charcoal and the powdered calamine were added. Heated calamine produces a zinc vapour that reacts with the copper, transmuting it to brass in a process called cementation. Archaeological finds dating back to the thirteenth century suggest Theophilus had good knowledge of how the material was made at that time – a process that only changed gradually and remained more or less unchanged during the high and late Middle Ages, invisible for the craftsmen to see and incomprehensible

In his book on minerals, Albertus Magnus attempts to explain the soul of brass.

for others trying to comprehend the process. However, the development of the industry in the later Middle Ages suggests the craftsmen did understand the process much better than one would imagine, reading Albertus Magnus. Perhaps the brass founders were not keen on sharing their trade secrets.

The cementation process was used for the production of brass until the late eighteenth century. New production techniques were introduced at a time when an industrial revolution was taking place in England; the process as described by Theophilus was finally abandoned in the nineteenth century. Before the development of a brassmaking industry in the Avon valley near

Above left: Brass lavabo kettle, fifteenth century. This liturgical object hangs in a niche in the chancel and was used to rinse the priest's hands before conducting mass.

Above right: Brass candle sticks, for both ecclesiastical and domestic use, were produced in large quantities in late medieval Dinant.

Bristol, the raw materials for producing brass, as well as latten objects, were imported. Several of the early Tudor latten eagles can be found only a short distance from Lynn – a major port that had intensive trade relations with Flanders. Yet, not only would objects be imported, so too were the ingredients, especially the calamine, which was a component that had to be retrieved from the continent. This stone was found in abundance in the small duchy of Limbourg, located between Liége and Aix-la-Chapelle in modern-day Belgium.

It is known brass objects were made in England during the Middle Ages. Perhaps the best known example is the funerary monument for Richard de Beauchamp made by William Austin and Bartholomew Lambespryng, a goldsmith. Both working in London, the fifteenth-century memorial in St Mary's Church, Warwick, is one the finest in England. The production of brass, however, seems to have been on a modest level, therefore not meeting domestic demand. As such, many objects like candlesticks or kettles for both domestic and liturgical use came from modern-day Belgium. Dinant, on the River Meuse, probably had some kind of royal prerogative for the exclusive sale of latten utensils at the Stalhof in London. A dependency of imports from the continent was considered a potential weakness during the reign of Henry VIII. Efforts were taken to retrieve calamine in England. During the Elizabethan era, there had been attempts to develop brass production in England after positive finds in the Mendips; however, a first attempt in 1568 to produce workable brass failed. From the seventeenth century onwards, Bristol became the English brass capital and it is little surprising several lecterns of the period found their cradle here. As the production became more and more industrialised, the cementation process as described by Theophilus in the early twelfth century was still used. This changed dramatically during the Industrial Revolution, when the cementation process was finally abandoned.

A brass eagle lectern was not made in one piece. It is assembled from up to eighty individually cast pieces using a lost wax technique. The bird itself usually consists of eleven pieces: two wings, two groups of four talons, and the body. Some eagles have an autonomous head. A model was made of plaster, clay or wood, from which moulds were taken. To make the moulds good quality clay is needed, so centres for brass-making are found on rivers, which doubles as a trading route. Initially the lost wax technique was used, but later templates were introduced; the latter being suggested by the simplified designs of the column and circular pedestal, which were introduced in the fifteenth century. It is known candlesticks were produced

At Southwell Minster, the lectern is dated 1503. (Photography David Iliff)

serially at that time. Known craftsmen of lecterns such as Jean Joses of Dinant or Guillaume Lefevre of Tournai have also produced candleholders. The casting techniques used for the production of columns and pedestals of the lectern and candleholders are very similar. Today it is thought the early modern lecterns were partially made using templates, which would mean serial reproduction of at least parts of the lectern much earlier in history than traditionally thought. William Borroughes in the late seventeenth century certainly did use the same model to take the moulds from – the eagles at Canterbury and Lincoln really are two birds of a feather. However, the others were made individually. The production of eagle lecterns remained a craft until the Industrial Revolution, ultimately resulting in mass production in the late Victorian Period.

To give more detail, like feathers on the wings, the pieces can be chiselled. Many lecterns are engraved, often recalling the name and date of the benefactor. From the Peterborough lectern of the late fifteenth century up to the early Georgian example in Brasenose College, the bookstand is inscribed. The dedication and engraving of the Maecenas is a recurring theme in the history of lecterns.

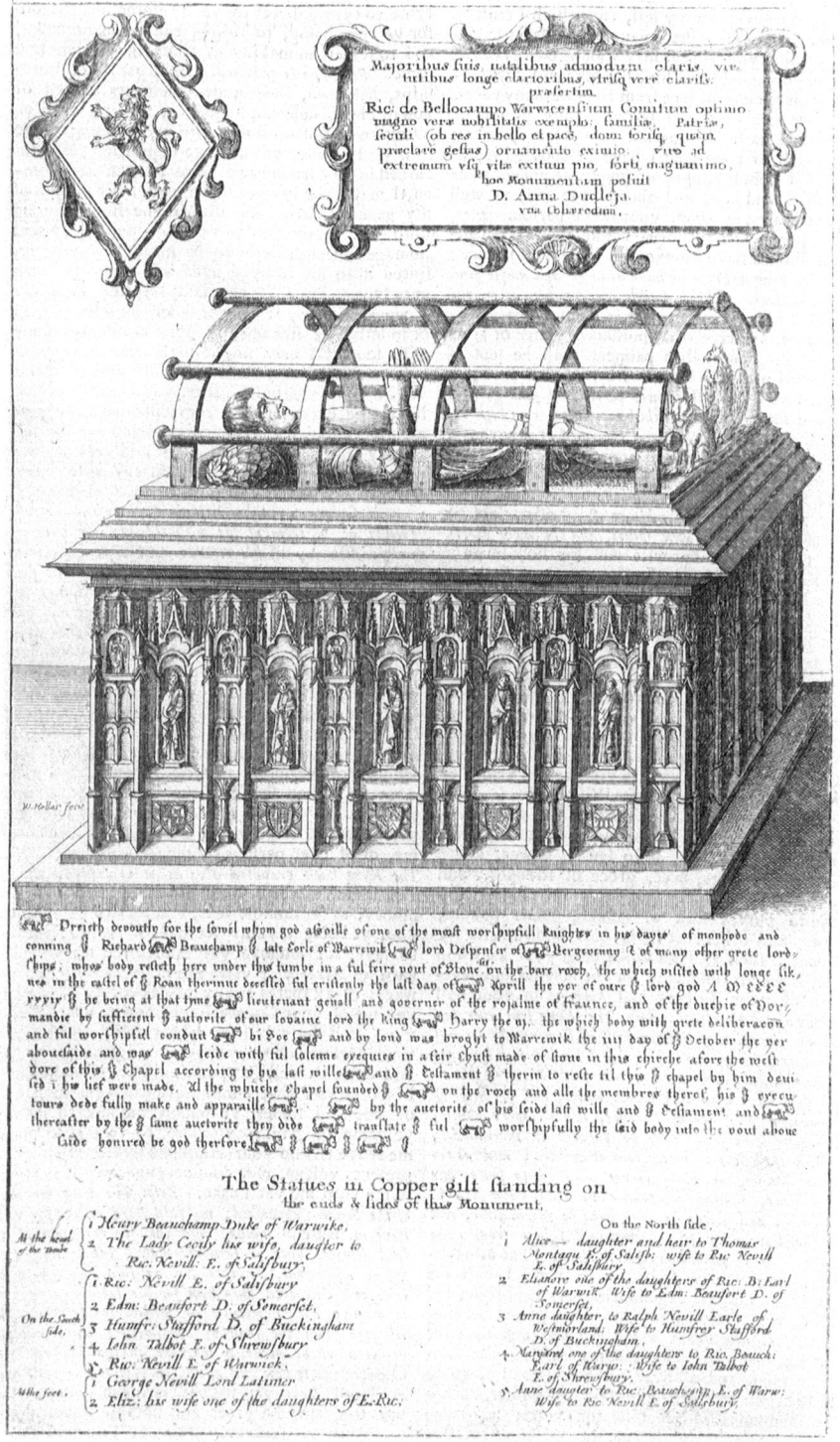

The memorial of Richard de Beauchamp, 13th Earl of Warwick, in the Collegiate Church of St Mary, Warwick.

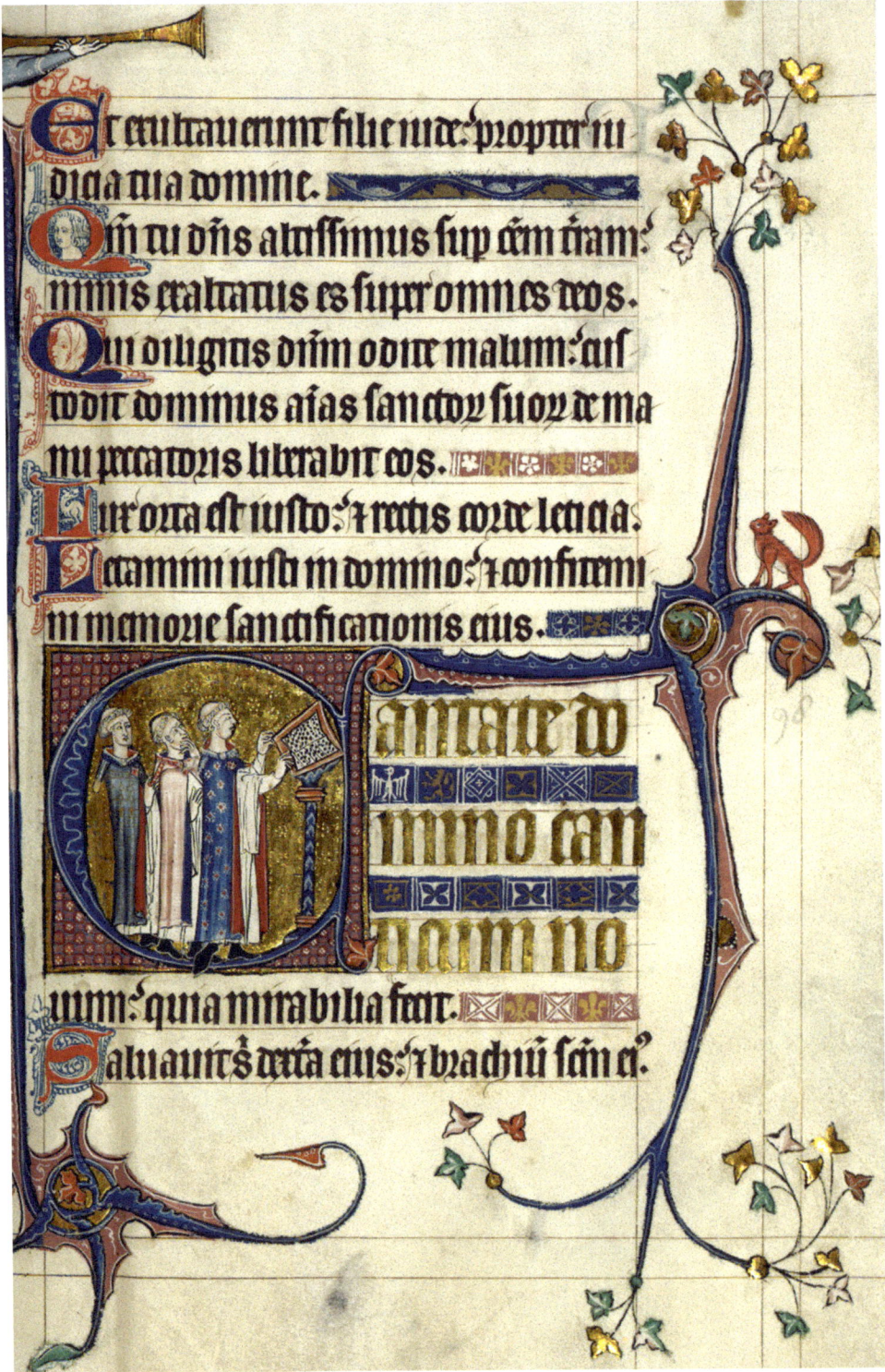

Medieval monks singing, East Anglian, fourteenth century.

Peterborough Cathedral, looking east. Photography David Iliff

Brass Eagle Lecterns in England

St Hugh's choir, Lincoln.

At Canterbury Cathedral, the principal house of worship of the Anglican Church, the present eagle lectern is a replacement of the latten bookrest bestowed to the Cathedral by Prior Thomas Goldson in the early sixteenth century. It was destroyed in the early days of the English Civil War by Colonel Sandys's troops in August 1642. Its replacement was made in 1663 by William Burroughes or Boroughes of London. Identical to the eye, the eagle in Lincoln Cathedral – donated by Johne Gooche and dated from 1667 – is also from his hand. As the Chapter of Lincoln wrote at the time, 'Most of the cathedrals escaped total destruction, yet many of them miserably rent, torn, defaced.'

After the Civil War and the iconoclasm of Puritanism that came with it, several churches and cathedrals in the country were in a piteous state. Numerous eagle lecterns were thrown away and others were veiled from Oliver Cromwell's troops. Years passed before the people of Cropredy, Oxfordshire, retrieved their latten eagle from the River Cherwell, where the early Tudor bookstand was hidden before the battle at Cropredy Bridge – or did the Parliamentary soldiers throw the shiny object considered a blasphemous idol in the river, as is told in Oundle, Northamptonshire? Puritans wanted to clean the church of Images, and the brass eagle was regarded as a golden calf. The lectern was recovered from the River Nene in the nineteenth century, when the river was dredged. Missing talons are said to have be taken by Cromwell's men. The origin of this late fifteenth-century lectern is believed to be Fotheringhay, however. The collegiate church of St Mary and All Saints is still considered a prominent Yorkist mausoleum. Following the Dissolution in 1553, the chancel, where the bookstand would be located, was pulled down.

Two lecterns in the Devon countryside are only a few miles apart, outside Newton Abbot. Both lecterns of Bovey Tracey and Wolborough were hidden from Parliamentary soldiers during the Civil War. In 1646 a battle took place at Bovey Heath, resulting in a victory for Cromwell. The lecterns remained secure in the woods and were recovered much later. The Wolborough bird lost its talons, but they were later replaced by ones made of silver. At Peterborough Cathedral a double-branched candlestick was ripped from the eagle lectern by Cromwell's soldiers during the Civil War. It is one of two described in the inventory of 1539 and is today one of the oldest latten bookstands in the country. The original engravings are difficult to encipher but have been recorded in earlier times. Abbot of Peterborough William Ramsey and Prior John Malden presented the lectern to the Abbey Church. This must have been somewhere between

Early modern eagle, Bovey Tracey. (Photography Justin Kroesen and Regnerus Steensma)

1471 and 1496. Today the eagle of Peterborough is one of few that has been at the same church for over five centuries, even before the church was elevated to cathedral status. Others' lecterns came into the church much later. Southwell Minster got its magnificent brass eagle lectern in the early nineteenth century. After some two and a half centuries hidden in a pond at Newstead Abbey, it was discovered after Lord Byron, great uncle of the poet, had the lake drained. The brass bookrest was auctioned and acquired by Sir Richard Kaye, prebendary of Southwell, and ultimately donated to the Minster in 1805. It is dated 1503 and is thought to have been made in Tournai, Belgium. Similarities to the eagle in Oxborough, Norfolk, are remarkable and inspired a recent restoration of the latter. Dated 1498, this lectern is engraved, revealing its donator as Thome Kypping. It is almost identical to the one in Wiggenhall St Mary, which has an unpolished lectern inscribed and dated 1518. The engravings recall Robert Barnard or Bernard, a Franciscan friar at Walsingham Priory, as the benefactor. Before the Reformation, Walsingham was the most important Marian shrine in East Anglia, attracting many pilgrims including Edward I and Henry VIII. The Edwardian inventory of 1552 describes two latten bookrests in the parish church, probably originating from the Priory after its destruction in 1538. Some argue the lectern in Wiggenhall must be one of those mentioned in the inventory. However, it would be customary at the time for benefactors to present these kinds of memorials to their native parish.

At Wimborne Minster, the early modern tradition of presenting a brass lectern as a commemoration is revived by Anthony Wayte. His crest and initials are engraved on the bookstand, which is still located in the vicinity of his and his wife's grave. It fits beautifully within the refurbishing of the collegiate church in 1610, when stalls and a rood screen were added. Only a few miles from Walsingham, a late fifteenth-century lectern was retrieved from the Norfolk marshes, supposedly in 1831. Today the eagle rests in the Victorian church of St Nicholas in Wells-next-the-Sea. According to legend it was thrown in by, or hidden from, Parliamentary troops during the Civil War. The fens of Cambridgeshire have been the hiding place for the Isleham lectern until its rediscovery in the early nineteenth century. Its origin is unclear and covered in obscurities. It either has relations to the local priory or Pembroke College, or was it brought to the church by one of the vicars in the early seventeenth century, who had been students at Cambridge. Research of casting techniques has revealed none other than the eagles of Dubrovnik and Florence as its relatives. Its date is the last quarter of the fifteenth century.

The eagle lectern in Oxborough, Norfolk, is engraved revealing the name of its benefactor, Thome Kypping, and the date of its production, 1498.

At that time the Peyton family contributed to the embellishment of the local St Andrew's Church; it could well be the one mentioned in the Edwardian inventory of 1552.

The lectern in Little Gidding, Huntingdonshire, was part of a decoration scheme in the seventeenth century. After the more austere Elizabethan Church, the beautification of the ecclesiastical space regained interest. Named after William Laud, the Archbishop of Canterbury and fervent promotor of the beauty of Holiness, this revival of the liturgy and consequent redecoration of the ecclesiastical space is called the Laudian Revival. Nicholas Ferrar acquired a latten lectern with a reading desk shaped like an eagle to complete the Laudian vision of the church interior. Ferrar had been at Cambridge University, where at that time four old eagle lecterns were at college chapels. Another pre-Reformation eagle lectern found a new home in Gloucestershire. Sir Baptist Hicks bestowed a reading desk to the church of Chipping Campden in 1618. A mercer in Cheapside, the later Viscount Campden may

In St Nicholas' Church, Dereham, the lectern dates back to 1482.

King's Lynn is the home of two early brass eagle lecterns. One can be found inside the Minster Church of St Margaret.

Early sixteenth-century lectern inside King's Lynn Minster.

have bought it in London. The church of St Christopher-le-Stocks in the City of London sold their brass eagle in 1581. Only a year later, one was acquired by the eighth Earl of Northumberland for the chapel at Petworth House, Sussex; it is unpolished and can be dated around 1500. At the time several church wardens sold off what was thought to be superfluous – only a simple reading desk was required for a Calvinist service. Several lecterns were obtained in the seventeenth century, like the one in Little Gidding, and some are falsely dated as a consequence. In Oxford, the lectern at Balliol College is engraved commemorating its donation to the college chapel, but it was made much earlier. It is the only English eagle to wear a crown and was made in the same workshop as the lectern in Urbino – curiously another crowned brazen image. The latter was acquired for the library of Federico da Montefeltro and was made in the late fifteenth century.

Christ's College in Cambridge was refounded by Lady Margaret Beaufort in 1505. The lectern with feet in the shape of greyhounds, emblem of the Beaufort family, also dates from this period. (Photography David Iliff)

Lady Margaret Beaufort in prayer.

Not lions but three greyhounds support the pedestal of the latten lectern in Christ's College, Cambridge. The close observer notices a colour difference, indicating these hounds were not made together with the rest of the bookstand. Greyhounds refer to the Beaufort family and it is believed this eagle lectern was a gift from Lady Margaret Beaufort, who re-founded the college in 1505. Recalling the pious nature of Lady Beaufort, an eagle to support the Bible appears to be a perfect object of remembrance.

Saint Paul's Cathedral was rebuilt by Wren after the destruction of the Great Fire of 1666. The recently finished interior required a new lectern, which was made in 1719 by Jacob Sutton of London. A few years earlier he had done the now-lost lectern for Salisbury Cathedral, giving an impression of how the eagle looked like. The stand is very baroque in treatment and the bird is possibly the best attempt to cast an eagle in brass in England, at least until the Victorian Age. Older representations of the interior show a pulpitum supporting the organ and the eagle lectern standing proudly in the choir, but both views are lost today. The Great Fire destroyed much of London, including many churches. One of the best-known designs by Sir Christopher Wren is St Bride's in Fleet Street. Many will be surprised to find one of his finest church interiors houses a brass eagle lectern dating back to the early 1500s that not only survived the flames, but also the bombs of the Second World War. A companion for this war survivor can be found in Coventry. Much of the historic centre was lost, including St Michael's Cathedral, which was replaced by Sir Basil Spence's remarkable creation. The early modern eagle lectern can be found in Trinity Church, one of the finest medieval parish churches in the country. Much has been preserved of the pre-Reformation, providing an interesting view of the ecclesiastical interior around 1500. The bookstand was cast by the same founders as the eagle lectern in St Martin's Church, Salisbury. A dedication to St Martin often indicates an old foundation. Today the church is largely fifteenth century. An early twentieth-century rood screen in the Oxford Movement tradition is a fitting background to the latten eagle.

The eagle in St Giles' Church, Norwich, is dated 1496 and originally stood in St Gregory's. An inscription in Latin reads: *Orate pro animabus Willim Westbrok Rose et Johanne uxorum eius* – 'Pray for the souls of William Westbrook and his wives Rose and Joanne' – on a bookstand that doubles as a memorial, and recalls the ascending eagle as a promise of resurrection. The Norwich eagle lectern is one of several, in England and abroad, with an inscription starting with *Orate pro anima(bus)*. Relocating the latten

Wiggenhal St Mary Magdalen, Norfolk. The lectern is dated 1518 and was presented by a Robert Bernard. According to some, it was originally in Walsingham Priory.

The Cathedral Church of St Nicholas, Newcastle upon Tyne. The early sixteenth-century brass eagle lectern would deserve a more prominent location.

The Tudor lectern in the Church of All Saints in Croft, Lincolnshire.

York Minster, looking from the lectern towards the choir stalls.

bookstand to another church also happened in Bristol. The eagle today in St Stephen was originally in St Nicholas. It was made in the same workshop as the lectern in the Anglican cathedral of Newcastle upon Tyne, also dedicated to St Nicholas, the patron of merchants and sailors. Casting techniques have revealed they were manufactured in the same workshop as the eagle lectern in St Mark's, Venice. During the seventeenth century, Bristol established itself as the brass capital of England. An early testimony of the craftsmanship can be found inside the church of St Mary Redcliffe.

By many regarded one of the finest parish churches in the country, the ecclesiastical space is beautified by a fine eagle lectern dated 1638. Almost half a century later, during the Restoration, two other lecterns were cast in Bristol. The latten eagle made for Bristol Cathedral had a tough fate. First it was rejected from the church it was made for, then, nearly sold as scrap metal in 1801, a new home was found at St Mary-le-Port, which lies now in ruins due to the bombings of Bristol during the Second World War. For many years the eagle was buried in the crypt of St John-on-the-Wall, but very recently the team of the Churches Conservation Trust is taking care of the poor bird. It is very similar to the lectern in York Minster, dated 1686. Four lions couchant support a brass square, upon which the pedestal and stand rest. This stand is delicately designed and very different from the contemporaries made in London.

From the high Middle Ages, the brass eagle lectern had become a regular piece of furniture for cathedrals. At Exeter, the latten bookstand replaced an older wooden version. Dating back to the fourteenth century, this lectern can now be admired at St Thomas. An extraordinary brass lectern stands in Norwich Cathedral; disregarded in the seventeenth century, it was dug up in the early nineteenth century and finally restored in 1841. Three orders of priesthood were added in the form of figures – a deacon, a priest and a bishop. The bird itself is picking its breast, symbolising Christ's sacrifice. Only a handful of these pre-Reformation pelican lecterns are known and the one in Norfolk is the only example in the British Isles. It was made in the late fifteenth century and shows strong similarities to the pelicans from Mechelen workshops. A similar example of this display of opulence can be found in St Amand's Church in Geel, Belgium.

At Croydon Minster, the lectern is in the nave and belongs to those eagles nicknamed Peter Pence's duck. It is part of a group of eagles of the early Tudor period that have their beaks open. Wiggenhall, Southwell Minster or Chipping Campden are but a few other examples. The story goes that the

Bristol is the home of two brass eagles dating from the seventeenth century. One is in St Mary Redcliffe.

The interior of St Mary Redcliffe, Bristol, as it appeared in *Cathedrals, Abbeys and Churches of England and Wales*, published in 1891.

The eagle lectern made in 1683 for Bristol Cathedral was nearly sold as scrap metal. After it was rejected from its former house of worship, the eagle lectern resided in the church of St Mary-le-Port, until the latter was destroyed during the Second World War. For decades the lectern remained hidden in the church of St John-on-the-Wall, where today this part of Bristolian heritage is being restored.

Choir of Bristol Cathedral.

open beak was intended as a money slot; an inventive strategy for collecting the money to build new St Peter's in Rome, bearing the mockery of reformists. In fact, the eagle lecterns prior to the Reformation were located in the chancel – the part of the church restricted for the clergy and inaccessible for the congregation – whereas money collectors would have been conveniently

Interior view of St Paul's Cathedral before the installation of the present baldacchino. The Georgian lectern had a prominent position addressing the congregation.

An early Tudor lectern, typical for the period.

located near the entrance of the building. Peter Pence's duck is part of the urban legends surrounding the Reformation. Recalling the moveable head of Folcuin's eagle at Lobbes Abbey, the open beak may have been used as an incense burner. In the Catholic liturgy it would be common practice to burn incense, in a censer, before and during Gospel reading. The depiction Villard de Honnecourt gave of an eagle lectern includes two figurines holding a censor. However, the author wants to stress that this hypothesis requires further research.

Some of the wealth of the medieval merchants can still be seen in the heritage of King's Lynn. The lectern in the Minster Church of St Margaret is the only one surviving of originally three bookstands. If the early modern lecterns were made abroad, the port of King's Lynn would have been the likely spot they arrived on English soil. Several examples exist within a relatively short distance of this medieval trade hub; Croft in Lincolnshire, and Upwell and Outwell in Norfolk are but a few examples. In Croft, two of the three little lions were stolen in 2008. Following the theft new lions

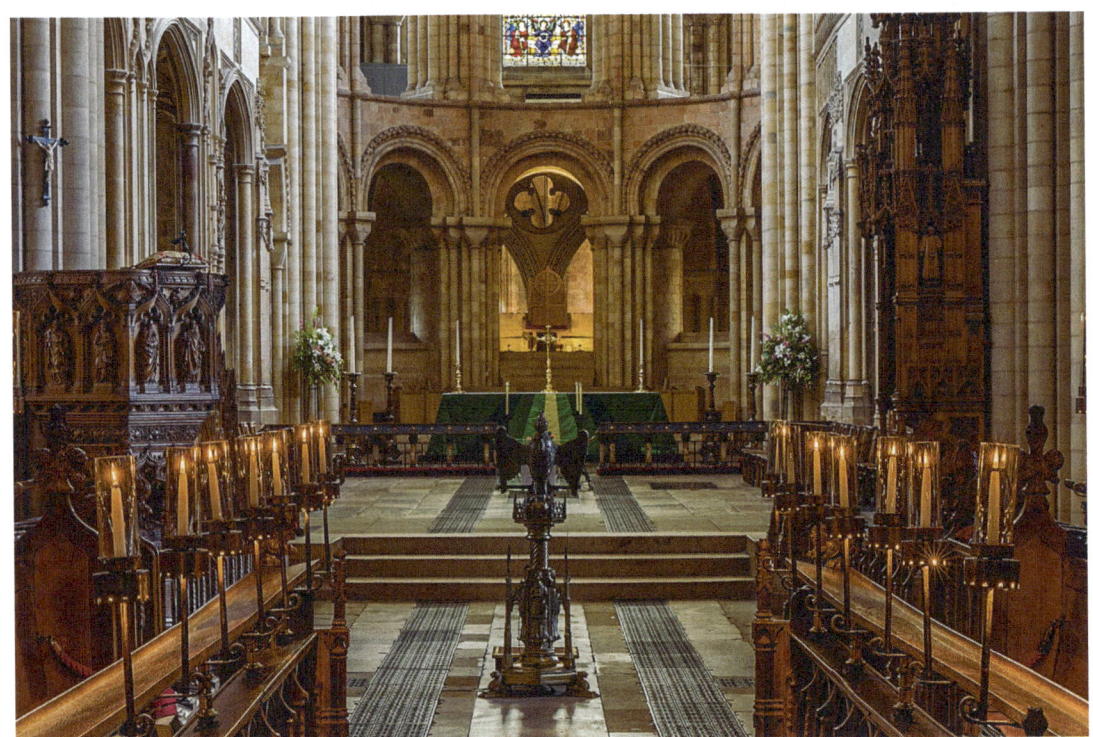

The late fifteenth-century pelican lectern inside Norwich Cathedral. It was restored in the nineteenth century when the stand received the three statues.

In Christian iconography a bird picking its breast is called a pelican and is a symbol for Christ's sacrifice.

Norwich Cathedral, chancel and spire.

were cast. A symbolic seven years later, the original pieces emerged at a car boot sale and thanks to modern techniques, the buyer explored their origin. Today the three lions are reunited in All Souls' Church.

In the fine interior of Walpole St Peter is a lectern that feels perfectly at home in this gothic interior. It is an impressive late fifteenth-century church, demonstrating the wealth of the region in early Tudor period. In Snettisham, Norfolk, the fourteenth-century decorated church was redone by the architect Frederick Preedy and a pre-Reformation brass eagle lectern, said to be recovered from the churchyard, regained its place in this lovely interior. Most of the church interior of St Margaret's in Lowestoft is also late Victorian; the latten lectern of 1504 endured and can still be admired. The eagle in Long Sutton, Lincolnshire, comes from the same workshop as the lecterns in Lowestoft and Coventry and can be dated to around 1500. The church of St Nicholas in East Dereham, Norfolk, is largely fifteenth-century, with many fittings dating to the late 1400s, including the magnificent Seven Sacraments font. The lectern is dated 1482 and was made in Liège, it is rumoured. In St Nicholas' Chapel in King's Lynn is an unpolished eagle from the fifteenth century very similar to that of Billingford, Norfolk, not only for the lack of polishing. The birds are not bad and share parallels to the one in Peterborough Cathedral. Both can be dated as late fifteenth-century. Unpolished today, these objects were intended to be brightly shining, as contemporary texts illustrate. Reignold Chirche of Bury postulated in his will of 1498 that his son Thomas 'do make clene the grete lectorn that I gave to Seynt Mary Chirche q'art'ly as long as he lyveth'. Yet, the patina can be pleasing as an understated reminder of its age.

In Redenhall, Suffolk, the word of God is supported by a rare double-headed eagle. This is unique in the British Isles and only a few others occur in Europe. A similar one originally in a monastery in Crete was relocated to Venice when the Turks took over the island. The double-headed eagle has been used as a royal crest for many realms, and is an image that goes back as far as the Assyrian empire. As mentioned before, in Christian iconography the image can be interpreted as a symbol of Christ's double nature as both human and divine, or as King of Heaven and Earth. Cavendish – one of the prettiest places in Suffolk – houses a provincial eagle-shaped bookrest in the church of St Mary. It is related to the lecterns in Woolpit and Croft and can be dated as early sixteenth-century. In the nearby village of Clare there is another one, said to be made in Flanders and a gift from Elizabeth I. Instead of seated lions, the pedestal is supported by collared dogs. These dogs may reveal the story of this lectern, just like the greyhounds of Christ's College in Cambridge are silent witnesses. The lectern in Woolpit was one of the last made before the beginning of the English Reformation and dates from 1520. It probably stood inside the Chapel of Our Lady of Woolpit until its destruction in 1551. The pilgrimage to the venerable Lady of Woolpit was very popular during the fifteenth and early sixteenth century, attracting even royalty.

The Brasenose eagle in Oxford concludes a cycle of college chapel lecterns, which started with the Laudian bookstands for Exeter College in 1637 and Magdalen College in 1633. The latter was given to the college chapel by Frewen, its president, and has leaf scrolls instead of little lions as feet. During the Restoration the William Borroughes of London produced three lecterns – the first being for Queen's College, Oxford. Borroughes' lecterns appear to reconnect to the examples of the Early Modern period. The stands are conceived as columns and decorated with geometrical motives and the eagle is a reconnection with the early modern examples, its open beak a diagonal line, its wings spread in the appearance of flight. Engraved are the words *Aquila Regina Avium* – 'The eagle is queen of the birds' – in a reference to the college's name. In 1691 the lectern for Wadham College, Oxford, was presented by Sir Thomas Lear. The quality of the eagle is in no relation to the fine pedestal and stem, which echoes the candelabras of the period. The last eagle lectern to be cast in England for at least a century was made for Brasenose College. It was bestowed by Thomas Lee Dummer in 1731. With it a period of college lectern donations and beautification of the church comes to an end, before the revival some hundred years later. By then the production of brass had changed dramatically, the medieval cementation process had become a thing of the past, and techniques changed during the Industrial Revolution.

The earliest example of a brazen bird in England – a beautiful product of medieval craftsmanship dating from around 1400 – can be found in Southampton. After the bombings of Southampton in 1940 it has found refuge in St Michael's, where it enjoys the company of a younger bird dating back to the late fifteenth century. A large triangular pedestal is supported by three seated lions, with the eagle ready to ascend to heaven. Like so many other of the early eagle lecterns it was originally part of a monastic interior, supported the manuscripts in Latin and assisted in the daily worship until the Dissolution of the Monasteries. Life in the abbey of Holy Rood came to a sudden end; yet the eagle lectern was given a new life after its initial redundancy and is today a memorable testimony of religious heritage in England.

Magdalen College Chapel, Oxford. (Photography David Iliff)

Origin of the Late Medieval and Early Modern Lecterns

The lectern made in Tournai around 1500 in St Martin's Church, Avelgem. (Photography Vincent van der Meulen)

Special attention is deserved for the bookstands of the late fifteenth and early sixteenth century. An astounding forty or so brass eagle lecterns described in this book can be dated between the Battle of Tewkesbury and the start of the Reformation. Compared to only two dating back to the Georgian Period and a handful to early Stuart times, the number of the early modern fixtures is significant. A production of nearly one every year, including the lost lecterns, the output was rivalled only in the late Victorian period. Dated in a maximum range between 1471 and 1543, possibly not extending half a century, these brazen birds are often called the English Lecterns. Bristol and London were the cradles of the seventeenth- and eighteenth-century eagle lecterns and there is little doubt the medieval bookstands were imported from the continent. A thriving trade between England and regions like Flanders was not limited to corn or wool and many luxury objects were manufactured for trade and crossed the borders. Monumental brasses for memorials were imported from Tournai, whereas the alabaster retables from Nottingham were all the rage in the Low Countries. Famously the church of Tongerlo Abbey was adorned with a retable from Nottingham in the early sixteenth century. Wooden lecterns were imported to England from Gdansk in modern-day Poland, which was was known for its high-quality oak.

The question of origin of the pre-Reformation lecterns in England was not raised until after the Great War, when Charles C. Oman published his article on the English Lecterns in the *Archaeological Journal*. Apart from the bookstands in England he also refers to some similar examples from Italy and Croatia, creating the notion of English Lecterns. Based on their striking likenesses, dating and predominant geographical location, the idea these brass bookstands were made in East Anglia is launched. The argument against a production in modern-day Belgium, known to have been one of the leading centres for brassmaking around 1500, is based on stylistic differences. A comparison to the Avelgem lectern, made in Tournai around 1500, illustrates this. The stand and eagle are unlike their contemporary counterparts in England, although the argument that Flemish eagle lecterns feature little demons between the bird's paws is refuted. A possible candidate for the English brass lecterns was presented by Charles C. Oman as a certain Reignold Chirche of Bury, bell founder. Brassmaking techniques of the period, however, link the manufacture of lecterns to that of candleholders, whereas bell founding is associated with the production of cauldrons and vessels. Both the lectern and the

Nottingham alabaster, the Adoration of the Magi.

Origin of the Late Medieval and Early Modern Lecterns

Above: Avelgem eagle lectern. (Photography Vincent van der Meulen)

Right: The early sixteenth-century lectern from Ste Croix, Liège, with a little demon.

The eagle lectern in Our Lady's Basilica, Tongeren, made by Jean Joses of Dinant.

candleholders in Our Lady's Basilica in Tongeren, Belgium, are made by Jean Joses of Dinant in the late fourteenth century, and in the fifteenth century Guillaume Lefevre of Tournai was the craftsmen of several Paschal candleholders – some with an attached desk for displaying books – and the eagle lectern in Halle, Belgium.

Then the architect Jean Squilbeck recovered a document in some Florentine archives, stating that the two brass eagle lecterns donated to the church of Ss. Annuziata in Florence, considered to be part of the English Lecterns, were made in Germania. Were the English lecterns made in Germany? Probably not. The location should be interpreted as the area known as Germania by the Romans, comparable to the contemporary use of Italia, centuries before the foundation of the unified Italy. Germania Inferior is more or less what was later called the Low Countries in English. An argument for a production in East Anglia had been the geographical location of many brass eagle lecterns of the fifteenth and early sixteenth century. Although the provenance of several lecterns is unclear and some arrived decades if not centuries after they had been made, the origin of the bookstands in Cavendish or Little Gidding remains unidentified, and the fact remains most brass eagle lecterns from the period are located in the eastern counties. A recusant aristocracy can be an explanation of why more than in other regions in England these fittings survived the cleansing of the ecclesiastical space during the Reformation. Norfolk is particularly rich in pre-Reformation church fixtures, including several seven sacraments fonts, which some explain by the position the Dukes of Norfolk held. Perhaps it is more accurate to stress the importance of King's Lynn at the time as one of the most important trading ports of England. A surprisingly large number of the brass lecterns can be found at a reasonable travelling distance from this medieval trading hub, and the wealth of the region in the early Tudor period.

More recently the casting techniques of several English lecterns have been studied. Not one but several workshops have been the cradle of these fittings, revealing a remarkable resemblance to the casting techniques used in Tournai and Dinant. Tournai had been a centre for the manufacture of ecclesiastical fittings since the twelfth century, when the vast Cathedral of Our Lady of Flanders was constructed. The baptismal fonts – enormous objects in the typical blue-grey marble of the region – even found their way into some English churches, notably Winchester Cathedral. Brasses, the memorials, made in Tournai were exported via Bruges and Ghent and adorn many churches in England. Both fourteenth-century memorials in King's Lynn were made in Tournai. The earliest recorded lectern was made for the cathedral in the first half of the thirteenth century, around the time Villard de Honnecourt drew his sketch for those who want to make an eagle lectern. Stylistically, Dinant is the likely cradle for the Holyrood lectern in Southampton, which can be compared to the lectern made by Jean Joses for St Catherine's in Houffalize. Both date from the late fourteenth century. However, the other English lecterns were probably not made in Dinant as in 1466 the town on the River Meuse was sacked by Charles of Charolais, the future Duke of Burgundy.

The trade wars against the principality of Liège had their desired effect and many craftsmen renowned for their superior brassmaking techniques relocated to cities in the Burgundian states. Some went downstream to Maastricht, where the impressive lectern that later adorned Pugin's Cathedral of St Chad, Birmingham, is presumed to have been made. Others set up shop closer to the international markets of Bruges and Antwerp, following in the footsteps of their twelfth-century townsmen who founded the brassmaking traditions of Tournai and Mechelen. Today it is suggested the town of Middelburg, between Bruges and Sluys, could have been the production place of the English Lecterns. Pieter Bladelin, Lord of Middelburg, had attracted brassmakers from Dinant to his new town. During his exile in Bruges, King Edward IV awarded Pieter Bladelin a privilege for the sale of brass objects in England. The earliest date given for the English lecterns is exactly the year Edward IV restored his throne – 1471. Made in Middelburg by craftsmen originating from Dinant and sold at the market in Bruges, they arrived in England through the ports of King's Lynn. Or did the wandering brassmakers cross the channel? In the sixteenth century the Strangers migrated to Norwich, fleeing religious persecution. A reversion of the influx of Englishmen who took refuge in the Low Countries during the Rose Wars. John of Gaunt, the first Duke of Lancaster, was born at St Bavo Abbey, Ghent – the celebrated sanctuary of the Flemish capital. For centuries craftsmen and artists have relocated to the markets; settling in London or East Anglia would be a valid option. A recent study of the residue found inside the brass eagle lecterns has shown they were made either in western Belgium or southern England.

The origin of the English lectern remains unclear. During the short period between the end of the Rose Wars and the break with Rome starting the

St Margaret's Church, King's Lynn.

English Reformation, a remarkably large amount of eagle-shaped lecterns were produced; the start of this incredible manufacturing was as sudden as the abrupt end. A single metalworking tradition is highly likely – not only stylistically, but also technically the similarities are striking. Although the origins of these brassmaking techniques reveal a strong connection to Tournai and Dinant, the place of production remains unclear. The mutual stylistic affinities between the eagles in England is significant, whereas there are none with the ones found in Flanders. An exclusive production for export is a possibility considered by some; perhaps the specimens in the Low Countries became victims of the iconoclasms of 1566 and the Puritan cleansing of the church interior that followed. The significance, however, of this group of English Lecterns is not in the location of its workshops, but rather the astounding amount manufactured in a period of only a few decades and their unique uniformity in design as expressed in the similarity of the columns and the pedestals.

Retrieved from a pond at Newstead Abbey, the early sixteenth-century lectern feels comfortable inside Southwell Minster. (Photography David Iliff)

Conclusion

A centuries-old brass eagle lectern looks down the choir inside Southwell Minster, witnessing the daily dance of clergy and visitors, locals and tourists. It feels at home in this house of worship. The early sixteenth-century lectern only arrived in the cathedral church of Nottinghamshire in the early nineteenth century. It was presented by the Dean of Lincoln, who

Newstead Abbey, Nottinghamshire.

had purchased this object at an auction. Lord Byron, a great uncle of the poet, had found it when the pond at his family home was drained, which was surely a surprise as for maybe two centuries the latten bookstand had been on the bottom of the lake. Hidden, rescued from destruction, dragged from its home of Newstead Abbey, the visitor's guide of Southwell Minster mentions Tournai in Belgium as its place of manufacture, made in 1503. From Peterborough Cathedral, where the lectern has been since it was presented to the abbey church over 500 years ago, to the church of St James in Chipping Campden, which received the eagle as part of a beautification of the church interior in the early seventeenth century, the brass bookrests with their proud eagles are testimonies of English history, scattered all over the country.

Over time this object has become a quintessential part of the Anglican church interior. Its origin goes back over a thousand years. The firm place it has today developed over several centuries, struggling in Puritan periods and revived by High Church movements. Many brass eagle lecterns are products of the Gothic Revival. In Thoverton, Devon, the latten lectern by W&J Cooper of 1841 is a convincing copy if the original at St Nicholas' Chapel in King's Lynn, Norfolk. It was even considered pre-Reformation by Charles C. Oman in his famed article, although he later rectified this understandable mistake. Before the English Reformation a church could have up to three lecterns, placed in the chancel (the part of the ecclesiastical space reserved for the clergy, secluded from the rest by a screen or pulpitum): one lectern for displaying the Gospel, another for reading the Epistle and a third for putting the musical books on. Under Elizabeth I a lectern had become the bookstand displaying a chained copy of the Bible in the English language. For all people to consult, it was placed centrally in the church, often in front of the pulpitum or screen. The brass eagle lectern, originally part of the liturgical furnishings, could be reused, yet many were sold. After the more austere Elizabethan Church, the Laudian Revival endorsed beautification of the ecclesiastical space. Little Gidding becomes a little laboratory for the Anglican church interior and a brass eagle lectern is part of its fixtures. Even the Puritan cleansing of the ecclesiastical space could not permanently eradicate this supposed idolatry. Restoration after the Commonwealth meant a renovation of the church interior; the casting of a new eagle lectern for Canterbury Cathedral is symbolic. Many lecterns doubled as memorials and are inscribed, revealing the benefactor's name. The early modern examples have the words *Ora pro anima* engraved on

An advert for Hart, Son, Peard & Co. Ltd, makers of brass eagle lecterns and other church fittings.

The Victorians even produced ecclesiastical fittings in series. This lectern could be St Giles-without-Cripplegate in London, St Edmundsbury Cathedral, Holy Trinity in Guildford, Surrey, or St Mary Magdalene's Church in Bridgnorth, Shropshire.

Lions couchant on a late Victorian lectern.

the pedestal. In the early Georgian Period the tradition comes to an end. Today the brass eagle lectern is primarily used for reading from the scriptures and as a minor pulpit. It is either placed at the crossing, or centrally between the choir stalls; in this, St Bride of Fleet Street is typical.

The latten bookstand consists of three parts: the stand, the pedestal and the reading desk shaped like an eagle. Often the stand is a column decorated with geometrical forms, and the pedestal is supported by three or four feet, often shaped like little seated lions. The bird with its wings widespread has its paws on a sphere. Some appear to be resting, others floating through the sky. In Christian iconography the eagle has multiple connotations. St John the Evangelist, writer of the first Gospel, is represented by an eagle. But it can also be a reference to the resurrection and ascension of Christ. The image of an eagle on a pole with widespread wings was a symbol for victory since Roman times.

Brass is an alloy of copper and zinc. Until the seventeenth century zinc as a material was unknown in the western world and the powder of a zinc containing stone called calamine was used. This stone was found in abundance in Vielle Montagne in modern-day Belgium. Medieval scholars

Above left: A more basic eagle lectern, with wings spread to support the Gospels, standing on a simple pedestal topped with a globe.

Above right: A more elaborate design for an eagle lectern, standing on a much more detailed pedestal that includes candleholders.

like Albertus Magnus treated brass with some mystery and the production process as a form of alchemy. Craftsmen of the Meuse towns developed an industry of brass objects that were traded all over Western Europe. The production of liturgical objects like the Paschal candleholder and the lectern remained a skilled craft, and these luxury objects were expensive. Medieval latten bookrests in England were cast in modern-day Belgium, whereas the seventeenth-century examples were made in London and Bristol. The origin of the early modern brass lecterns remains largely unknown. Some of the workshops may have been located near Bruges, where the luxury goods were traded on the emerging arts market. Immigrants from the Low Countries, taking with them their skills, may have manufactured these lecterns in London or East Anglia. The output of these lecterns of the late fifteenth and early sixteenth century was only rivalled by the Victorians. Their mass-produced furnishings filled the Anglican churches of an Empire. Some original work was done by people like Sir George Gilbert Scott and Francis Skidmore, whose creations adorn some cathedrals and great churches. These mobile fittings have been relocated over time, from the chancel to the nave and back to the choir, looking east and looking west. Their wings have carried the word of God for centuries. Hand-written in Latin or printed in English, the eagles have supported good news in all circumstances, adorning the interiors of the great cathedrals, college chapels and parish churches of England.

Exeter College Chapel, Oxford.
(Photography David Iliff)

List of Brass Eagle Lecterns

Medieval
01 Southampton (Hants.), St Michael's Church, originally in Holy Rood Abbey

Early Modern
02 Norwich (Norf.), St Giles' Church, 1496.
03 Longton Sutton (Lincs.), St Mary's Church.
04 Oundle (Northants.), St Peter's Church.
05 Cropredy (Oxon), Church of St Mary the Virgin.
06 Coventry (West Midlands), Holy Trinity Church.
07 Wolborough (Devon), St Mary's Church.
08 Southampton (Hants.), St Michael's Church.
09 Lowestoft (Suff.), St Margaret's Church, 1504.
10 Little Gidding (Cambs.), St John's Church.
11 Wells-next-the-Sea (Norfolk), Church of St Nicholas.
12 Salisbury (Wilts.), St Martin's Church.
13 Southwell (Notts.), Southwell Minster 1503.
14 Newcastle (Tyne and Wear), Cathedral of St Nicholas.
15 Bristol, St Stephen's Church.
16 Oxborough (Norf.), St John's Church, 1498.
17 Oxford, Balliol College Chapel.
18 King's Lynn (Norf.), King's Lynn Minster (St Margaret's).
19 Petworth (W. Sussex), Petworth House Chapel, bought in 1582.
20 Exeter (Devon), Exeter Cathedral.
21 Walpole St. Peter (Norf.), St Peter's Church.
22 Clare (Suff.), St Peter and St Paul's Church.
23 Redenhall (Norf.), Church of the Assumption of the Blessed Virgin Mary.
24 Peterborough (Cambs.), Peterborough Cathedral, 1471–1496.

25 East Dereham (Norf.), St Nicholas' Church, 1482.
26 King's Lynn (Norf.), St Nicholas' Chapel.
27 Isleham (Cambs.), St Andrew's Church.
28 Upwell (Norf.), St Peter's Church.
29 Croydon, Greater London, Croydon Minster (St. John Baptist).
30 Snettisham (Norf.), St Mary's Church.
31 Cavendish (Suff.), St Mary's Church.
32 Cambridge (Cambs.), Christ's College Chapel, 1505–1510.
33 Bovey Tracey (Devon), Church of St Peter and St. Paul.
34 Croft (Lincs.), Church of All Saints.
35 Outwell (Norf.), St Clement's Church.
36 Wiggenhall St Mary Magdalen (Norf.), Church of St Mary Magdalene, 1518.
37 Billingford (Norf.), St Peter's Church.
38 Woolpit (Suff.), St Mary's Church, 1520.
39 City of London, St Bride's Church, around 1500.
40 Chipping Campden (Glos.), St James' Church.
41 Norwich (Norf.), Norwich Cathedral, pelican lectern around 1500

Early Stuart / Laudian Revival
42 Wimborne Minster (Dorset), Minster of St Cuthberga, 1623.
43 Oxford (Oxon), Magdalen College Chapel, 1633.
44 Oxford (Oxon), Exeter College Chapel, 1637.
45 Bristol, Church of St Mary Redcliffe, 1638.

Restoration
46 Oxford (Oxon), Queen's College Chapel, made by William Borroughes, 1662.
47 Canterbury (Kent), Canterbury Cathedral, made by William Borroughes, 1663.
48 Lincoln (Lincs.), Lincoln Cathedral, made by William Borroughes, 1667.
49 Bristol, originally in the Cathedral, now St John-on-the-Wall, Bristol, 1683.
50 York (N Yks.), York Minster, 1686.
51 Oxford (Oxon), Wadham College Chapel, 1691.

Georgian
52 St Paul's Cathedral, City of London, made by John Sutton, 1719.
53 Oxford (Oxon), Brasenose College Chapel, 1731.

BIBLIOGRAPHY

Barnwell, P. S., Harper, Sally & Williamson, Magnus, *Late Medieval Liturgies Enacted: The Experience Of Worship In Late Medieval Cathedrals And Parish Churches:* Routledge, 2016.

Lehmberg, Stanford E., *Cathedrals Under Siege: Cathedrals in English Society, 1600–1700:* The Pennsylvania University Press, 1996.

Brownsword, R., English *pre-Reformation Eagle Lecterns*, Journal of the Antique Metalware Society, Vol. 6: 1998, pp. 7–16.

Day, Joan, *The Continental Origins of Bristol Brass*: 1984.

de Ruette, Monique, *Les Lutrins 'anglais': considerations techniques*, Actes. Congres de la Federation des Cercles d Archeologie et d Histoire de Belgique, Vol. 49: 1991, pp.71–81.

de Ruette, Monique, *Les Lutrins coulés en laiton au moyen âge et à la Renaissance*, In: Hermal, P. & Pacco, M. (eds) *Art du Laiton Dinanderie,* Société Archéologique de Namur: 2005, pp. 95–103.

Didier, R., *Lutrins et statuaire en laiton du pays Mosan au Moyen Age*, (eds) *Art du Laiton Dinanderie,* Société Archéologique de Namur: 2005, pp. 63-94.

Oman, C. C., *Medieval Brass Lecterns in England*, Archaeological Journal, Vol. 87: 1930, pp 117–149.

Oman, C. C., *English Brass Lecterns From The Seventeenth And Eighteenth Centuries*, Archaeological Journal, Vol. 88: 1931, pp. 218–227.

Rehren, Thilo & Martinon-Torres, Marcos, *Naturam ars imitata: European Brassmaking between Craft and Science, Archaeology, History and Science: Integrating Approaches to Ancient Materials:* Left Coast Press, 2008, pp. 167–188.

Ryrie, Alec, *Worship and the Parish Church in Early Modern Britain*: Routledge, 2013.

Spraggon, Julie, *Puritan Iconoclasm During the English Civil War*: Boydell Press, 2003.

Squilbeck, Jean, *Les Lutrins dinantais de Venise et de Gênes*: Palais des Academis, 1941.

Thomas, Nicolas & Bourgarit, David, *Le laiton produit en masse au Moyen Agee*: La Recherche, 2012.

Thomas, Nicolas & Plumier, J., *Cuivre, laiton, dinanderie mosane: Ateliers et productions métallurgiques à Dinant et Bouvignes au Moyen Âge (XIIIe–XVIe siècles)*, Archéopages, hors-série, Archéologie sans frontières: 2010, pp. 142–151.

van der Meulen, Marcus, *Those Flemings Were Getting Everywhere!*: conference presentation, Vicenza, 2016.

van der Meulen, Marcus, *The Brass Age: Fifteenth and Early Sixteenth Century Eagle Lecterns from Flanders and Tournai*: symposium presentation, King's Lynn, 2016.

van der Meulen, Marcus, *Brass Eagle Lecterns in England*, Historic Churches, Vol. 26: 2017.

Wellington Gahtan, Maia, '*The 'Evangelistario' from the Cathedral of Messina*, The Journal of the Walters Art Museum, Vol. 59: Focus on the Collections (2001), pp. 59–72.

Whiting, Robert, *The Reformation of the English Parish Church*: Cambridge University Press, 2010.

Southwell Minster choir, Nottinghamshire.

Left: Hereford Cathedral with the Victorian screen by Scott & Skilmore. A brass eagle lectern was placed in front. Photograph taken late nineteenth century.

Below: Little lions support the bookstand at St Bride's in the City of London.